101 Scriptures to Help You
Talk to God Each Day

Prayer 101

Learn to talk to God
When you need **help**

TIM DILENA

TIMES SQUARE ▣ CHURCH

Presented to

From

Date

"Call to Me and I will answer you..."
—Jeremiah 33:3, NASB

Published by Carpenter's Son Publishing
www.christianbookservices.com

Printed in United States of America

ISBN: 978-1-956370-89-8

Cover Design by Hybrid Studios

Interior Design by Hybrid Studios

"But You Said..."

Quoting God to God: That's How We Really Pray

There is an often overlooked but very important prayer in the book of Genesis. It is a prayer of a man who was in crisis. His name was Jacob, and he was about to face a 20-year-old problem. That problem's name was Esau. Esau was Jacob's brother, and their relationship was destroyed by Jacob's deceit and stealing decades earlier. And without any warning, Jacob found out that he and his brother were on a collision course to meet each other. The last time Jacob was with his family, he was told that Esau wanted to hurt him. That is the last thing that was in Jacob's head. Knowing this back story, Jacob prayed this prayer:

"But You said, 'I will surely do you good, and make your offspring as the sand of the sea, which cannot be numbered...'" (Genesis 32:12, ESV)

Jacob didn't pray for victory. He didn't pray that they would avoid each other. Jacob's prayer was built on 3 words. Those first three words were what makes this prayer and any prayer powerful. Jacob said, **"But You said..."** Jacob was quoting what God had said to him 20 years earlier in Genesis 28. Jacob's prayer was quoting God's Word back to Him.

"But You said" is the response to a crisis. It's the prayer of a man that has no idea what this encounter with his brother will be like. It is a lesson on **how to face your battles with prayer and God's Word and believing for God's intervention.**

"But You said" is not challenging God, rather it is challenging your situation by praying God's Word into it. Jacob wasn't challenging God's Word; he was putting God's Word into his prayer and into the mess he created.

Jacob's prayer changed the encounter. Why would Esau be bringing 400 men with him if his intention was simply to give his brother a hug and let bygones be bygones. You don't need 400 men for that!

After Jacob prayed, after Jacob quoted God's Word back to God, God intervened. Genesis 33:4 (NASB) says, "Then Esau ran to meet him and embraced him, and fell on his neck and kissed him, and they wept." Who would have expected that?

Powerful prayer is when you can say to God, "But You said." "But You said" is our authority in prayer.

The **power in quoting** God to God is that it appeals to the **veracity of God**. The **veracity of God** means **God always tells the truth**. Another way to say it is that **God cannot lie** (Hebrews 6:18; Titus 1:2). God will always be true to what He has said, whether it was 20 years earlier or 2000 years earlier.

Jacob quotes God's own words back to Him like a child would quote something their parents have said to them. It was as if Jacob knew **God will always keep His Word**. This is why **reading the Bible each**

day helps you pray more effectively. God always responds to His Word.

1 John 5:14-15 (NASB} says, "This is the confidence which we have before Him, that, if we ask anything according to His will, He hears us. And if we know that He hears us in whatever we ask, we know that we have the requests which we have asked from Him."

His will is found in His Word. So when you ask according to His Word, He hears us. Always remember the Bible is God's Word. When the Bible speaks, God speaks. So quoting the Bible in prayer is actually quoting God in prayer. Effective prayer is praying the Word of God back to God.

Let's take a page out of Jacob's prayer as he faced his crisis. As you read these verses during your prayer time, declare like Jacob, **"But You said." Quote God to God.**

You hold in your hand 101 Bible promises with which you can say to God, "But You said." You can say these words knowing God always keeps His word. People have told me, "When I pray, I don't know what to say." This little book is the answer to that question. If you are wondering what to say in prayer, simply quote God to God. You will face situations where people will say things, your mind will say things, circumstances will even say things, but that's when you get on your knees and tell God, **"But You said."**

DIVE DEEPER

Watch the message that inspired this book

Discover the power of saying "BUT YOU SAID" if you want God to listen to your prayer.

Scan this QR code
or visit **tsc.nyc/butyousaid**

Table of Contents

When I need
Hope in the fight

Psalm 34:17 (NASB)
"The righteous cry, and the Lord hears and delivers them out of all their troubles."

Isaiah 54:17 (NASB)
"No weapon that is formed against you will succeed."

1 John 4:4 (KJV)
"Greater is He that is in you, than he that is in the world."

Isaiah 59:19 (NKJV)
"When the enemy comes in like a flood, the Spirit of the Lord will lift up a standard against him."

Romans 8:31 (NKJV)
"What then shall we say to these things? If God is for us, who can be against us?"

Notes

But You said this... about hope in the fight.

When I need **Healing**

Isaiah 53:5 (NKJV)

"But He was wounded
for our transgressions,
He was bruised for our iniquities;
The chastisement for our
peace was upon Him,
And by His stripes we are healed."

Exodus 23:25 (NIV)

"Worship the Lord your God,
and His blessing will be on your
food and water. I will take away
sickness from among you."

Psalm 30:2 (NIV)

"Lord my God, I called to You
for help, and You healed me."

Jeremiah 17:14 (NIV)

"Heal me, Lord, and I will be healed;
save me and I will be saved,
for you are the one I praise."

Hebrews 13:8 (NIV)

"Jesus Christ is the same
yesterday and today and forever."

Notes

But You said this... about healing.

When I need
Protection

Proverbs 18:10 (NKJV)

"The name of the Lord is a strong tower; The righteous run to it and are safe."

Psalm 121:7–8 (NIV)

"The Lord will keep
you from all harm–
He will watch over your life;
The Lord will watch over
your coming and going
both now and forevermore."

Hebrews 13:5b–6 (NKJV)

"For He Himself has said,
'I will never leave you nor forsake you.' So we may boldly say:
'The Lord is my helper;
I will not fear. What can man do to me?'"

Psalm 34:7 (NIV)

"The angel of the Lord encamps around those who fear Him,
and He delivers them."

Psalm 91:11 (NKJV)

"For He shall give His angels
charge over you,
To keep you in all your ways."

Proverbs 1:33 (NIV)

"But whoever listens to Me
will live in safety and be at ease,
without fear of harm."

Isaiah 43:2 (NKJV)

"When you pass through
the waters, I will be with you;
And through the rivers,
they shall not overflow you.
When you walk through the fire,
you shall not be burned,
Nor shall the flame scorch you."

Notes

But You said this... about protection.

When I need
Provision

Philippians 4:19–20 (NASB)
"And my God will supply all your needs according to His riches in glory in Christ Jesus. Now to our God and Father be the glory forever and ever. Amen."

Ephesians 3:20 (NKJV)
"Now to Him who is able to do exceedingly abundantly above all that we ask or think, according to the power that works in us."

Proverbs 11:25a (NASB)
"The generous man will be prosperous."

Proverbs 19:17 (NASB)

"One who is gracious to a poor man lends to the Lord,
And He will repay him
for his good deed."

Proverbs 3:9–10 (NIV)

"Honor the Lord with your wealth, with the firstfruits of all your crops; then your barns will be filled to overflowing, and your vats will brim over with new wine."

Notes

But You said this... about provision.

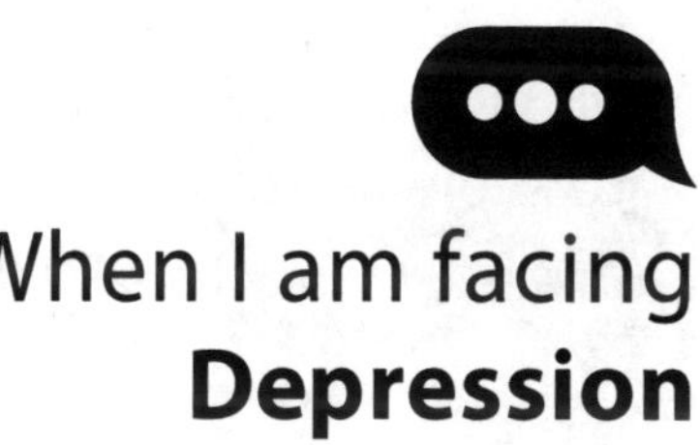
When I am facing
Depression

Psalm 34:18 (CEV)
"The Lord is there to rescue all who are discouraged and have given up hope."

Lamentations 3:20–23 (CEV)
"That's all I ever think about,
and I am depressed.
Then I remember something
that fills me with hope.
The Lord's kindness never fails!
If He had not been merciful,
we would have been destroyed.
The Lord can always be trusted
to show mercy each morning."

Isaiah 41:9–10 (NLT)

"I have called you back from
the ends of the earth, saying,
'You are my servant.'
For I have chosen you
and will not throw you away.
Don't be afraid, for I am with you.
Don't be discouraged,
for I am your God.
I will strengthen you and help you.
I will hold you up with my
victorious right hand."

Psalm 143:7–8 (NLT)

“Come quickly, Lord,
and answer me,
for my depression deepens.
Don’t turn away from me,
or I will die.
Let me hear of your
unfailing love each morning,
for I am trusting You.
Show me where to walk,
for I give myself to You.”

Psalm 9:9 (NLT)

"The Lord is a shelter for the oppressed, a refuge in times of trouble."

Psalm 30:5b (NLT)

"Weeping may last through the night, but joy comes with the morning."

Notes

But You said this... about facing depression.

When it's hard for me to **Rest & Sleep**

Proverbs 3:24 (NIV)
"When you lie down, you will not be afraid; when you lie down, your sleep will be sweet.

Psalm 3:5 (NIV)
"I lie down and sleep;
I wake again, because the Lord sustains me."

Matthew 11:28 (NIV)
"Come to Me, all you who are weary and burdened, and I will give you rest."

Psalm 4:8 (NIV)

"In peace I will lie down and sleep,
for You alone, Lord, make me dwell
in safety."

Psalm 127:2 (NIV)

"In vain you rise early
and stay up late,
toiling for food to eat—
for He grants sleep to
those He loves."

Notes

But You said this... about rest & sleep.

When my **Mind is Troubled**

Philippians 4:8 (KJV)

"Finally, brethren, whatsoever things are true, whatsoever things are honest, whatsoever things are just, whatsoever things are pure, whatsoever things are lovely, whatsoever things are of good report; if there be any virtue, and if there be any praise, think on these things."

Isaiah 26:3 (NKJV)

"You will keep him in perfect peace,
Whose mind is stayed on You,
Because he trusts in You."

2 Thessalonians 3:3 (NKJV)

"But the Lord is faithful, who will establish you and guard you from the evil one."

Colossians 3:2–3 (NKJV)

"Set your mind on things above, not on the things that are on earth. For you died and your life is hidden with Christ in God."

John 14:1 (NASB)

"Do not let your heart be troubled; believe in God, believe also in Me."

Notes

But You said this... about being troubled.

When I can't break a **Stubborn Habit**

2 Corinthians 3:17 (NIV)
"Now the Lord is the Spirit, and where the Spirit of the Lord is, there is freedom."

Psalm 119:45 (NIV)
"I will walk about in freedom,
for I have sought out Your precepts."

2 Corinthians 5:17 (NKJV)
"Therefore, if anyone is in Christ, he is a new creation; old things have passed away; behold, all things have become new."

1 Peter 2:16 (NASB)

"Act as free men, and do not use your freedom as a covering for evil, but use it as bondslaves of God."

Galatians 5:1 (NIV)

"It is for freedom that Christ has set us free. Stand firm, then, and do not let yourselves be burdened again by a yoke of slavery."

John 8:36 (NKJV)

"Therefore if the Son makes you free, you shall be free indeed."

Notes

But You said this... about a stubborn habit.

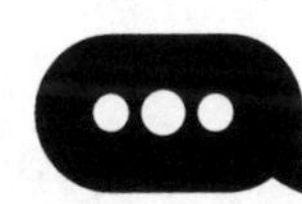

When **Worry & Anxiety** won't let me go

Philippians 4:6–7 (NIV)

"Do not be anxious about anything, but in every situation, by prayer and petition, with thanksgiving, present your requests to God. And the peace of God, which transcends all understanding, will guard your hearts and your minds in Christ Jesus."

Matthew 6:33–34 (NIV)

"But seek first His kingdom and His righteousness, and all these things will be given to you as well. Therefore do not worry about tomorrow, for tomorrow will worry about itself. Each day has enough trouble of its own."

1 Peter 5:7 (NIV)

"Cast all your anxiety on Him
because He cares for you."

Psalm 55:22 (NIV)

"Cast your cares on the Lord
and He will sustain you;
He will never let the
righteous be shaken."

Psalm 107:28 (NASB)

"Then they cried to
the Lord in their trouble,
and He brought them
out of their distresses."

Notes

But You said this... about worry & anxiety.

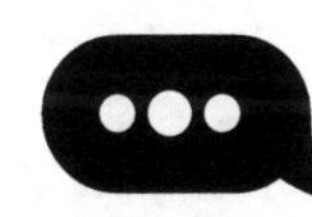

When I need the **Right Words**

Proverbs 16:21 (NASB)

"The wise in heart will be called understanding, and sweetness of speech increases persuasiveness."

Proverbs 17:28 (NASB)

"Even a fool, when he keeps silent, is considered wise; When he closes his lips, he is considered prudent."

Proverbs 15:1 (NASB)

"A gentle answer turns away wrath, but a harsh word stirs up anger."

Proverbs 15:2 (NASB)

"The tongue of the wise makes knowledge acceptable, but the mouth of fools spouts folly."

Proverbs 18:21 (NASB)

"Death and life are in the power of the tongue, and those who love it will eat its fruit."

Notes

But You said this... about needing the right words.

When I need the **Power of Prayer**

Jeremiah 33:3 (NKJV)
"Call to Me, and I will answer you, and show you great and mighty things, which you do not know."

Mark 11:24 (NKJV)
"Therefore I say to you, whatever things you ask when you pray, believe that you receive them, and you will have them."

Romans 8:26 (NASB)
"In the same way the Spirit also helps our weakness; for we do not know how to pray as we should, but the Spirit Himself intercedes for us with groanings too deep for words."

Matthew 7:7–8 (NASB)

"Ask, and it will be given to you; seek, and you will find; knock, and it will be opened to you. For everyone who asks receives, and he who seeks finds, and to him who knocks it will be opened."

Jeremiah 29:12–14a (NASB)

"'Then you will call upon Me and come and pray to Me, and I will listen to you. You will seek Me and find Me when you search for Me with all your heart. I will be found by you,' declares the LORD."

Notes

But You said this... about the power of prayer.

When I am in a **Difficult Environment**

Colossians 3:23–24 (NASB)

"Whatever you do, do your work heartily, as for the Lord rather than for men, knowing that from the Lord you will receive the reward of the inheritance. It is the Lord Christ whom you serve."

1 Peter 2:12 (NASB)

"Keep your behavior excellent among the Gentiles, so that in the thing in which they slander you as evildoers, they may because of your good deeds, as they observe them, glorify God in the day of visitation."

1 Peter 2:13–15 (NASB)

"Submit yourselves for the Lord's sake to every human institution, whether to a king as the one in authority, or to governors as sent by him for the punishment of evildoers and the praise of those who do right. For such is the will of God that by doing right you may silence the ignorance of foolish men."

Proverbs 16:7 (NIV)
"When the Lord takes pleasure in anyone's way, He causes their enemies to make peace with them."

Ephesians 6:7–8 (NASB)
"With good will render service, as to the Lord, and not to men, knowing that whatever good thing each one does, this he will receive back from the Lord, whether slave or free."

1 Peter 2:18–19 (NASB)

"Servants, be submissive to your masters with all respect, not only to those who are good and gentle, but also to those who are unreasonable. For this finds favor, if for the sake of conscience toward God a person bears up under sorrows when suffering unjustly."

Notes

But You said this... about a difficult environment.

When I need **Help Forgiving**

Proverbs 17:9 (NKJV)

"He who covers a transgression seeks love, But he who repeats a matter separates intimate friends."

Colossians 3:13 (NASB)

"Bearing with one another, and forgiving each other, whoever has a complaint against anyone; just as the Lord forgave you, so also should you."

Proverbs 19:11b (NASB)

"And it is his glory to overlook an offense."

Mark 11:25 (NASB)

"Whenever you stand praying, forgive, if you have anything against anyone, so that your Father who is in heaven will also forgive you your transgressions."

Ephesians 4:32 (NASB)

"Be kind to one another, tender-hearted, forgiving each other, just as God in Christ also has forgiven you."

Notes

But You said this... about forgiving.

When I need **Strength**

2 Corinthians 12:9 (NKJV)

"And He said to me, 'My grace is sufficient for you, for My strength is made perfect in weakness.'"

Psalm 73:26 (NKJV)

"My flesh and my heart fail;
But God is the strength of my heart and my portion forever."

Nehemiah 8:10c (NLT)

"Don't be dejected and sad, for the joy of the Lord is your strength!"

Philippians 4:13 (NASB)

"I can do all things through Him
who strengthens me."

Psalm 28:7–8 (NLT)

"The Lord is my strength and shield.
I trust Him with all my heart.
He helps me, and my heart
is filled with joy.
I burst out in songs of thanksgiving.
The Lord gives His people strength.
He is a safe fortress for His
anointed king."

But You said this... about strength.

When I need **Direction**

Proverbs 16:3 (NIV)
"Commit to the Lord
whatever you do,
and He will establish your plans."

James 1:5–6 (NKJV)
"If any of you lacks wisdom, let him ask of God, who gives to all liberally and without reproach, and it will be given to him."

Psalm 32:8 (NASB)
"I will instruct you and teach you
in the way which you should go;
I will counsel you with My eye
upon you."

Isaiah 30:21 (NASB)

"Your ears will hear a word behind you, 'This is the way, walk in it,' whenever you turn to the right or to the left."

Proverbs 3:5–6 (NKJV)

"Trust in the Lord
with all your heart,
And lean not on your
own understanding;
In all your ways acknowledge Him,
And He shall direct your paths."

Notes

But You said this... about direction.

When **Fear** is trying to control me

2 Timothy 1:7 (NKJV)

"For God has not given us a spirit of fear, but of power and of love and of a sound mind."

Proverbs 3:25–26 (NIV)

"Have no fear of sudden disaster or of the ruin that overtakes the wicked, for the Lord will be at your side and will keep your foot from being snared."

Isaiah 41:10 (NKJV)

"Fear not, for I am with you;
Be not dismayed, for I am your God.
I will strengthen you, Yes, I will help you, I will uphold you with My righteous right hand."

Psalm 23:4 (NKJV)

"Yea, though I walk through the
valley of the shadow of death,
I will fear no evil;
For You are with me;
Your rod and Your staff,
they comfort me."

Psalm 27:1 (NKJV)

"The Lord is my light and
my salvation; Whom shall I fear?
The Lord is the strength of my life;
Of whom shall I be afraid?"

Psalm 34:4 (NKJV)

"I sought the Lord, and He heard me, and delivered me from all my fears."

Notes

But You said this... about fear.

When I need a **Friend to Find God**

Acts 16:31 (NIV)
"They replied, 'Believe in the Lord Jesus, and you will be saved—you and your household.'"

Romans 10:1 (ESV)
"Brothers, my heart's desire and prayer to God for them is that they may be saved."

Ezekiel 11:19 (NLT)
"And I will give them singleness of heart and put a new spirit within them. I will take away their stony, stubborn heart and give them a tender, responsive heart."

Matthew 19:25–26 (NIV)

"When the disciples heard this, they were greatly astonished and asked, 'Who then can be saved?' Jesus looked at them and said, 'With man this is impossible, but with God all things are possible.'"

Galatians 4:19 (NLT)

"Oh, my dear children! I feel as if I'm going through labor pains for you again, and they will continue until Christ is fully developed in your lives."

Notes

But You said this... about a friend finding God.

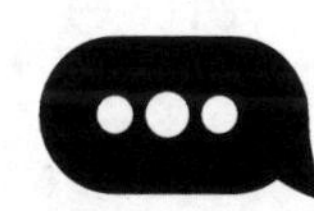

When I just need some **Help**

Psalm 121:1–3 (NLT)
"I look up to the mountains—
does my help come from there?
My help comes from the Lord,
who made heaven and earth!
He will not let you stumble;
the one who watches over
you will not slumber."

John 14:16–17a (NIV)
"And I will ask the Father, and
He will give you another advocate
to help you and be with you
forever—the Spirit of truth."

Psalm 46:1 (NIV)
"God is our refuge and strength,
an ever-present help in trouble."

Hebrews 4:16 (NLT)

"So let us come boldly to the
throne of our gracious God.
There we will receive His mercy,
and we will find grace to help us
when we need it most."

Psalm 54:4 (NLT)

"But God is my helper.
The Lord keeps me alive!"

Hebrews 13:6 (NIV)

"So we say with confidence,
'The Lord is my helper;
I will not be afraid.
What can mere
mortals do to me?'"

Notes

But You said this... about help.

When I need to know **God is in Control**

1 Corinthians 10:13 (NIV)

"No temptation has overtaken you except what is common to mankind. And God is faithful; He will not let you be tempted beyond what you can bear. But when you are tempted, He will also provide a way out so that you can endure it."

Job 42:2 (NLT)

"I know that You can do anything, and no one can stop You."

Joshua 1:9 (NLT)

"This is my command—be strong and courageous! Do not be afraid or discouraged. For the Lord your God is with you wherever you go."

Romans 8:28 (NLT)

"And we know that God causes everything to work together for the good of those who love God and are called according to His purpose for them."

Notes

But You said this... about God being in control.

One More Thing Before We Are Done

There is a story in John 4:49–54 (NASB) that saved a father's son from death that stirred my heart. It was how the miracle happened that caught my attention. A desperate father had a son on his deathbed, and he ran out of options. His title was "royal official" which meant he had access to every up-to-date medical treatment. But nothing worked, and his son's health continued to decline. With time running out on his little boy, this man chose Jesus as his last option. He needed a miracle.

The royal official asked Jesus to come personally to his home, but Jesus said, "No," because Jesus was going to do something unexpected. Jesus did not go to the child but sent His promise with the man.

"Go; your son lives" (v. 30).

For a man that probably never heard "No," this was epic. It was remarkable, not only to be told "No," but to then believe the promise he was given. These are the words that the man took with him as he journeyed home.

The man started back home, and the Bible says, "The man believed the word that Jesus spoke to him and started off" (v. 50). Those were the assuring words spoken to a desperate father, and they are encouraging words for us today.

The words of Jesus are as good and sure

for us today as they were for this father. I pray that you realize that you can take the Word of God with you and know there is life on the other side.

When the man returned home, he was met by one of his employees with the good news that his son was healed. The father asked when his son began to get better.

"Then they said to him, 'Yesterday at the seventh hour the fever left him'" (v. 52b).

"So the father knew that it was at that hour in which Jesus said to him, 'Your son lives'" (v. 53a).

The Bible then says, "He himself believed and his whole household" (v. 53b).

That's the power of Jesus' word. It was working way before the man got home. That is the power of trusting in God's promises.

We need a promise like that as we journey home. The home I am referring to is not where you reside presently but where you will reside eternally. To get to your heavenly home, Jesus has a promise for you right now that you can walk with all the way into heaven. Just as we borrowed the words of a desperate father who wanted his son healed in John 4, let's borrow the words that were given to a religious leader named Nicodemus in John 3.

What was at stake for this man was not his physical life, but eternal life. That was the bigger issue. Jesus gave him a promise to travel with, all the way to his heavenly home.

"Jesus replied, 'Very truly I tell you, no one can see the Kingdom of God unless they are born again'" (John 3:3, NIV).

Have you been born again?

This the most important question for you to answer in this life because what is at stake is eternity.

Jesus was describing to this religious man that just as a person has a first birth physically, you need a second birth spiritually. You need to be born again. How that happens is as simple as a child learning his ABC's. Let's use those 3 letters to describe what it means to be born again.

"A" stands for "Admit." You must admit that everyone is broken on the inside. You can't fix yourself. You have a condition called sin.

"B" stands for "Believe". The only way for your sin condition to be fixed is by believing. You must believe that God sent His Son to fix your sinful condition. He died the death you were supposed to die. He lived the life you couldn't live. And He has offered you a reward you don't deserve: forgiveness and heaven. Jesus became your sin bearer when He died on the cross.

Finally, **"C" stands for "Confess."** You must confess Jesus as Lord. Romans 10:9 (NASB) says, "If you confess with your mouth Jesus as Lord, and believe in your heart that God raised Him from the dead, you will be saved."

To confess Jesus as Lord is to say, "Jesus, You are in charge. You are in charge of every day, not just Sundays."

Jesus said when you pray you should say "Our Father" (Matthew 6:9). But remember, you can't call Him Father unless you are His child. And to become His child is not from physical birth but by a second birth—by being born again.

If you want to be born again, say this prayer from your heart. Let the words of Jesus about being born again be the journey words you take all the way into eternity.

Dear Lord Jesus,

I believe that You are the Son of God. I believe that on the cross, You took my sin, my shame, and my guilt; and You died for it. I believe that You faced hell for me, so I would not have to go; and You rose from the dead, to give me a place in heaven, a purpose on earth, and a relationship with Your Father. Today, Lord Jesus, I turn from my sin to be born again. God is my Father, Jesus is my Savior, the Holy Spirit is my Helper, the Bible is my guide, and Heaven is now my home. In Jesus' Name, Amen!

Conclusion

You have made the greatest decision of your life. There will be moments when you will think, "This is too good to be true." The good news is that it is true because God is truthful. When you face doubts about the decision you just made, here are some promises you can pray...

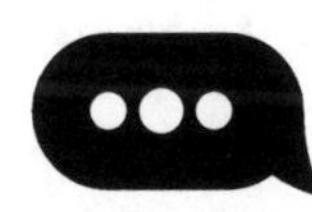

When I need **Assurance of Salvation**

Titus 3:5 (NIV)
"He saved us, not because of righteous things we had done, but because of His mercy. He saved us through the washing of rebirth and renewal by the Holy Spirit."

John 5:24 (NASB)
"Truly, truly, I say to you, he who hears My word, and believes Him who sent Me, has eternal life, and does not come into judgment, but has passed out of death into life."

Romans 10:9 (NKJV)

"That if you confess with your mouth the Lord Jesus and believe in your heart that God has raised Him from the dead, you will be saved."

Ephesians 2:8–9 (NKJV)

"For by grace you have been saved through faith, and that not of yourselves; it is the gift of God, not of works, lest anyone should boast."

Acts 2:21 (NIV)

"And everyone who calls on the name of the Lord will be saved."

But You said this... about assurance of salvation.

Notes

Notes

TIMES SQUARE ▣ CHURCH

1657 Broadway NY, NY 10019

tsc.nyc